Book of Poetry

Dr. Daniel Simon Pierre
Book of Poetry (I Shall Rise)

Published by BooxAi
ISBN: 978-965-578-198-4

Book of Poetry

I Shall Rise

Dr. Daniel Simon Pierre

Preface

This book is about all my original thoughts, ideas, feelings, and private emotions. Good and bad things have happened to me publicly and privately in my life.

I thank my wife for inspiring me - although most of my writing occured as a young and single man.

I think and know that the readers will be touched emotionally, relate to the parallelism expressed, and see themselves in my poems. My advice to the reader is not to read as they are driving; instead, relax, rest on a couch with a glass or Merlot or Chardonnet, elevate the feet, and grab one of my books to read. Yes, also remember to dim the light, and play classical music or soft rock in the background.

My intention is simply to keep it real, to touch every dormant nerve and emotion (good or bad), and to have the reader think of their past.

Lastly, I desire to connect to each of my readers on a personal, emotional, spiritual, psychological, and physical basis.

I love to write poems.

In Memoriam

Where are they now great men and women of the past?
That paved the way for us all

From Toussaint Louverture and Jean-Jacques Dessalines,
who set us free from the shackles of tyranny and slavery?

To those of old who built the great pyramids
and formulated the Pythagorean Theory,
from various descendants of mighty kings and great queens
and royalty of majesty to the queen of Sheba,
most beautiful queen of the East
from the kingdom of Axum in Ethiopia?

From the great Mahatma Gandhi,
also known as 'Ganghiji' and 'Bapu'
who suffered much pain, humiliation,
and tyranny in his own country, and fasted for
freedom and equality for his people and country?

To the humble and passionate
and non-violent civil rights leader Dr. Martin Luther King,
who paid dearly with his life,
and was martyred for the cause of justice and equality?

From Rosa Park, Edger Everett,
and all the martyred sons and daughters,
who demanded respect, fairness, equality,
and refused to give up their seats?

To the admirable
Nelson 'Khulu' Mandela,
who ultimately paid a great price
and sacrifice with his life
for more than 25 years?

And now finally to Barak Hussein Obama,
who knew that he could accomplish
the long-foretold dream and make it a reality:

'Yes, we can'

Rastafari

Rasta
Rasta man
Rasta man vibration positive

Bob
Bob Marley
Bob Marley and the Wailers
Jah Rastafari

Haile
Haile Selassie
Haile Selassie Emperor of Ethiopia and Prophet of the Rasta-
farians
Jah Rastafari

Ziggy
Ziggy Marley
Ziggy Marley and the Melody Makers
Jah Rastafari

Dread
Dreadlocks
Dreadlocks naturally groomed and uncut
Jah Rastafari

Roots
Ganja
Splits smokes by all true Rastafarians
Jah Rastafari

Claat
Bloodclaat
Bumboclaat
Raasclaat
Jah Rastafari

Reggae
Reggae music
Roots, rock, reggae, this is reggae music
Jah Rastafari

Fried dumplings, ackee and cod fish
Jerk chicken, pork, and fish
Oxtail, curry goat, fish escovitch, brown stew chicken run down,
pepper pot soup
Plum juice, Irish mush, and sorrel juice
Jah Rastafari

I Shall Rise

Risen from the pages of deceptions,
despair, and disappointments.
I shake up the dust of the past,
lifted my head above the clouds,
and gaze at the more hopeful and promising horizon.

Indeed, I am alone,
the worst has past and vanished away in thin air,
and the best is yet to come.

A new beginning is ushering at dawn,
for distant and unpleasant memories are gone.

I will rise to a new beginning,
to a new chapter without ending,
where life and the future will be sweeter,
forgetting of the past that made me so bitter.

Risen from the nightmares of my life,
to my destiny and what God has in store for me,
I shall rise.

Risen from the depth of poverty and my sad reality,
to fulfillment and victory,
I shall rise.

A seed or two of hope were implanted deep in me,
yet, I found myself alone and lonely to raise them,
I shall rise.

A bitter separation,
a nasty divorce or being a widow,
cannot hold me back,
because yet I shall rise,
I shall rise.

And even when I was rejected and misused,
mentally, physically, and/or emotionally abused,
I shall rise.

I shall rise
I shall rise
I shall rise

The Scorpion Lover

He pierced my tender heart with his sharp torn,
poison my vulnerable senses with seductive venom,
the love portion he alone uses to captivate his prey.

Entrapped in the snare of his love,
I found myself weak in his presence,
losing all control, reason, and good judgment.

I can't, I can't resist his powerful aura,
the aroma of sensuality overwhelmed my inner being,
privately and convincingly saying to myself, I want more.

Intoxicated by his charm and mannerism,
my knees buckled under the weight of his love
before I hit the floor,
not really understanding what just got over me.

My only desire now is to become his prey,
for him to do as he will, oh have mercy on me
wish me well, for I don't know what to expect.

This bowed-legged-masculine-hunk of a man,
gentle, charming, gallant.
Wow! I wonder how it would be?

He secures me firmly in his muscular arms,
embracing me with such passion and seduction,
caressing me endlessly before.

Finally kissing me with such tenderness,

my tongue intertwined with his in a labyrinth of love,
warm, fuzzy, and juicy it feels.

Losing control and no real desire to stop,
as a gush of oxygenated warm blood flows to my head,
I melted in his arms like dark rich chocolate.

Tears of joy running down my cheeks,
not bashful of the way I fell now or what the outcome may be,
wishing that this ecstatic joy that I'm experiencing
would last for eternity.

He moved, dinned me, and grooved me,
to the sound and rhythm of a sweet melody,
watching and making each calculating moves
with meticulous perfection,
surely summer as come,
for I surely feel quite warm and wet deep inside.

Oasis of Love

The desert of my life is dry, arid, and parch.

Sad and lonely nights have been constant in my life
passing and hanging over my head
like an immense black cloud of despair.
Trees naked without limbs, branches or even leaves,
no shades or covering.

Desolation, depravity, and the sad reality
but just when I thought dying of thirst was the only solution
you came into my life and brought me hope and joy.
The joy to live and survive the condition of my state of mine
I found that oasis of love in you.

Rounded shape of comfort makes me feel secure
dark rich soil for the new grass
to grow and the royal palm trees roots to anker.

Now finally, and finally now
the sparrows have a place to rest
fresh cool water to a base my thirst,
enough for the camels to drinks
before departing to their long journey
smooth and smooth bolder serving as sanctuary

Dr. Daniel Simon Pierre

Time

What is time? Even where is it? When shall we find it?
Is it just a mere pigment of our vivid imagination?
Or an endless continuum of infinite movement.

Is it purely seconds carefully adjusted by the expensive Timex?
Maybe consecutive minutes kept watchfully by the timekeeper.
Perhaps unaccounted hours lost in space each day seeking to make
amends.

From a to z, from zero to infinity,
found in the black hole or continuum of life.
In the twilight of space or in the twilight of the night.
Or twilight zone of time
And just like sands in an hourglass,
times keeps dripping away one at a time
Do we have enough of it? Even if we should?
Then what would we do?

Wave of ambiguous moments passing away,
but precious time remain constant.
The continuum of life in fact never ceases,
but flows through time.

For it is indeed profound, baffling, and dubious.
Time is of the essence, the essence of life itself.
For in the beginning it was, and in the end, it will be.
For indeed there is a beginning and surely an end.

The end of his world, or the end of time itself,
alone time is self-sufficient and endless,

reliable and never late, that is time!

As written in the good book, time is destining and appointed,
a time for every wish and season,
a time for every rhyme and reason.
So, I ask, do you have the time?

Field Negros

Strong, rugged, uneducated, brute, and unpolished.
Brash, wild, untainted, and unwilling to obey.
Ruff on the edges, muscularly hard.
Always trying to run away on each occasion.
Not wanting to be shackled, domesticated,
and controlled by the master's chains.
Rusted, tight to the ankle's bones.
Cutting to the marrow and oozing precious ancestral blood.
the blood of their forefathers flows deep within.
Inside all the veins of their foremothers
coming from the first over shipman of precious cargo.
Stacked high as packaged sardines for eminent delivery
to a land far away with no return address or an inquiry

House Negros

Refine, polish, and fair silky skin
Combed, straight, greasy, and partially curly brown hair
Educated, can spell, and read some easy lines
Controlled, calm, and behaves properly
Like sheep, docile, example and demonstration of proper
mannerism
'Yes, Sir', she answered politely,
with her head looking down at the stoned floor
as her masters' often called for choirs
and fetching some errands nearby.
To do all perfectly and meticulously before sundown
Belly distended by month's end, soon to reveal the identity
Light fair-skinned, straight hair, grey eyes baby,
seed fruit from the master's one prowling predatory night.
She was defenseless, couldn't say no,
not truly free, you know.
For she is regarded, just like the rest,
as possessions belonging to the plantation
Just like cattle or lives stocks,
priced daily to determine their value

Herald

Who is he, that good news who came into the world?
To save it from its perversion and destruction

To save the sins of all for all
So that all humanity can find salvation

Salvation found only in him through
the shedding of his precious blood
To purge, purify, save, and sanctify

To forgive, forget with no regret
That all man can and won't forget

The sacrifice of the lamb of God carried on Golgotha
Slayed on the rugged cross shamefully

Bleed to purify all humanity
And all those who believe in his name

Who is this bearded lamenting Jew?
His name is Jesus Christ of Nazareth

The Throne Room

Ushering the holly of hollies
There he sat on the throne of grace
Behold the perfect lamb of God
which took away the sins of the world.

So majestic, incorruptible, and shinning with holiness
The son of God, the Son of man, the Savior, the Messiah,
the lion of the tribe of Judah,
the lineage of David, the Christ, Jesus himself.

Standing before him the twenty-four elders
in worship and adoration:
to his right flank the cherubim
with their two edges flaming swords;
to his left flank the Serafin's
with two winds covering their feet,
two wings
covering their faces,
and two wings
hovering in his presence.

The righteous, the saints, the saved,
those who accepted him as their Lord and personal savior
and trusted in his message of salvation,
and those that tarry and
who kept the faith?

Were prostrate before his feet,
saying repeatedly in unison;

Holly, Holly, and Holly
is the Lamb of God,
who is seating on the throne?

Fall From Grace

Here we are, men and women of so-called integrity,
Here we are, standing on the throne of grace.
In the presence of all mighty God.

Spiritual hypocrites we are, God doesn't know us.

We wear our blue suits and white dresses
thinking we are holly,
Like old decrepit roaches
going on a shopping spree of sins.

Spiritual hypocrites we are, God never knew us.

Shopping for sins and pleasure, that is,
directed by lust, greed, and our inept inability
to resist temptation and the desires of the flesh.

Spiritual hypocrites we are, dogs depart from me, says God.

Steadfast in the word of our merciful God the father.
For God, he temps no one, for he can't be tempted.

Spiritual hypocrites we are,
our names are not written in the lamb book of life.

On Sundays, we come to church well-groomed
as if we were going to be wed;
and on Mondays, we commit adultery
with the church secretary or our neighbor's wife,
hastily preparing our funeral.

On Sundays, we mount the pew of salvation
as though it was our private business;
and on Tuesday we steal, rob the poor,
and the weak among us

On Sundays, we shoot praises and
thanksgiving with our holly lips;
and on Wednesdays, we curse and call our brothers
and sisters 'Raca'

On Sundays, we give God our offerings,
tidings, and gifts as good sacrifices;
and on Thursdays,
we sell drugs to our fellow men.

On Sundays, we clap our hands in joy
and render a handshake;
and on Fridays, we beat and abuse
our wives and children with those same hands.

On Sundays, we preach an inspired
apostolic message of salvation and redemption;
and on Saturdays, we break every rule, ordinance, law,
and commandment ever written.

Fall from grace, spiritual hypocrisy.

Poverty Was a Disgrace

Poverty was my name and I was a shame,
poverty was my name, but I wasn't the one to blame.

I was born in the ghetto of Harlem,
a place that I regretted being from.

Son of an illiterate and alcoholic father,
son of a whorish and irresponsible teenage mother.

There I was poor as I am,
who can free me I asked with pity.

My father was a sanitation worker with his bottle by his side,
my mother was pregnant and had me at thirteen.

I was born in poverty!

Their mediocre income was not enough to support us,
but they gave birth to four plus,
Shironda, Shemiqua, Sheniqua, and Latisha.

A cloud of poverty and despair hung over our heads,
Nothing to eat but some dry stale bread.

My father came home always drunk, dirty, and smelly,
My mother couldn't care for herself, dropped out, barefooted.

On welfare, receiving food stamps,
governments handouts and hand downs,
I guess my sisters were destined to follow in her footsteps;

Ugly, unable to control their raging hormones,
babies having babies.

I was born in poverty!

There I was, looking like a skeleton,
unable to support my own weight,
my stomach touched my spine,
dry bones uncovered by flesh showing.

Poverty smelled terrible!

I smelled like an old, humid piece of damp dirty rag,
my clothes were disheveled, and torn up.

They were worn out, patched up,
full of unwanted holes and missing bottoms,
many nights I slept on the cold and dirty floor.
Hungry, frightened, unable to shed a tear,
I was too weak to speak, too weak to scream;
sometimes I fainted when I could no longer take it.

I knew poverty!

We didn't own a damn thing,
We were too poor to afford anything.

The only thing we had coming,
food stamps, Medicaid,
and welfare checks on the first of the mount.

The mailman was our best friend,
only he could truly understand.

But when he was late,
he became our worst public enemy;
we dared him to call in sick or even think of missing his date

I knew poverty!

We live in the project housing in Manhattan,
A large ghetto city of no man's land.

Our one-bedroom shack,
was the worst in this stinking place.

It looked like an abandoned crack house,
A shelter for abandoned, stray, and lost animals.

Broken windows, old led paint peeling off the cracked walls,
the cold hardwood floor had enormous gaps.

Serving as a sanctuary for the uninvited fat rats,
infested with huge flying reaches, spider nests,
and prehistoric flies.

I hated poverty!

My neighborhood was filthy,
polluted with slimy worms and carcasses of dead
domesticated animals.
Oh! God, why me?

Trash piles and overflowing dumpsters line the sidewalks,
poodles of water ran the deserted streets,
mosquito lava erupted from the damp mud.
The residents were distraught, disfigured,

discourage, and lethargic.
Feeling sorry for themselves,
careless, shameless, and blameful of others.
There is no way out.

Crime, prostitution, theft, vandalism, drugs use,
and unemployment were at their peak;
We didn't own anything;
everything belongs to the slave masters,
the white man

I hated poverty!

I walked miles to school on an empty stomach,
tired, sweaty, dusty feet.

Use clothing, faded, and wrinkled,
smelling like mildew and roaches' nests.

Purchased from the thrift shop,
given by the Salvation Army.

Kids glared, laughed, and taunted me,
I didn't have any friends,
poverty was my only companion.

I was lonely, rejected, and impoverished,
my lunch was a dry peanut butter sandwich.

God save me from my misery!
What I have done to this world?
I often asked myself.

What I have done to this world?
For many nights I wasn't fed.
Was it the color of my skin?
Was I paying for my sin?

God, save me from my misery,
Life for me had no meaning;
A terrible, horrible, and humble beginning.

When I opened my eyes, poverty surrounded me.
When I tried to breathe, poverty penetrated me.
Thus, I talked, looked, and behave as a poor child.

Poverty was a disgrace!

What the future holds for me?
What must I do to be free?
Only God can deliver me,

Only God can give me a dream.

For me, poverty was a disgrace.

Dr. Daniel Simon Pierre

The Enemy Within

Who are you Mr. and Mrs. AIDS?
What are you?
Who conceived you?

Why are you so evil, destructive, and deadly?
Where do you belong? In hell perhaps!

What are you?
What made you?
Tell me, my enemy, how do you look?
You are an odious disease,
Destructive and devastating you are, oh AIDS!

Why do you treat me as such?
You infiltrated my body and made me weak
You traveled my bloodstream and infested me
You ate my substance

My bones are cancerous and fragile.
My flesh is rotten.
My skin is dry, flaky, and lumpy with painful sores.
Fouls odor overwhelm my surface.
You stole my hair for your canopy.
In me you seek your refuge, why?

I'm young, but my frame feels old.
I'm young, but my body is weak.
What must I do? But to wait!
Wait, for my fallen peak.

Congratulation

Roses are red,
And violets are blue

You love him,
And we are certain he loves you too

May the good Lord truly bless you both,
As you grow in spirit and truth

May the everlasting and unconditional love of God
mix with your love and keep you both
joined forever.

Again, congratulation on this exciting day,
and may God richly and gracefully bless you both.

God and Us

Two hearts, one love
Two tastes, one choice
Two ideas, one will
Two persons, one life
Two kids, one family
Two mistakes, one sin
Two sins, one forgiveness
Two destinies, one destination
Two deaths, one life
Two roads, one heaven
Two wrong decisions, one eternal burning hell
One Savior, one joyful eternal life
Thank you, God, for loving us
Thank you, Jesus, for saving us
Thank you for choosing us to dwell in paradise with thee

Motherland

Vast fields of lush dense greenery carpets the land
As the wild beast, lions, and giraffe runs freely.

Villages of haft naked and haft dressed nomads not ashamed,
To see the real, them as they were created.

Paid and purchased safari for pure amusement and for the kill,
Like the thrill to kill, in the rush of satisfaction

Hunts and shacks line the hillside, the ravines, and basins,
With echoes of joy or laughter resounding from the mountaintop.

Lions, king of the jungle,
predators and carnivores kill to eat,
unlike the white men and
uncaring foreigners who kill for joy,
assessment, and trophies.

Haiti: Pearle of the Antilles

Haiti is the precious first black free negro slave nation
of the Antilles
shinning bright like the biggest star far away in the firmament
high above the milky way eliminating the constellations.

Majestic royal tall palm trees lines
the sidewalk of Chant De Mars.
For the midday casual strollers
and merchants to find sanctuary from the scorching,
rays of the sun or for the hard-working women merchants
enjoying the last money exchange moment
and of a brief siesta.

Gorgeous white sand beaches, look like bright crystal
But smooth and soft under the soles of the American and
European tourists
Cabanas covered with dry old plantain leaves
Serving Five Star Barbancoo Rum on ice, soothing cremas,
and refreshing cool Coconut water,
which has just fallen from the porch partly unrouted tree.

Majestic iron and metal cruise ships from all over the world line
the ducks like infantry soldiers marching for battle.
Or as the indigenous Tainos entering their hunts
after a successful hunt.
Happy multiple ethnics, mostly Caucasians from the U.S
debarking from enjoying themselves,
purchasing low price artifacts from the country artisans.

Quabosal and The Iron Market
busting with business and exchange of currencies
from the tourists,
deals and bargains overheard across tables and countertops,
capturing the imagination of an art dealer or an auctioneer.

Dr. Daniel Simon Pierre

Haiti: Better Future Ahead

When the restavecs' dirty secret system ceases, a reasonable and
descent but conscientious minimum wage establishes,
then real change as come.

When natives no longer leave their beloved and
cherished homeland in droves
staked in commandeered unsafe boats and small vessels.
Exploited, purchased their boarding pass
to sail for the unwelcome and prestigious.
Shores of America, the so-called promised land,
then we have arrived.

When Haiti gets proper worldwide recognition
and respect fighting for
freedom and shading their crying blood of
justice and equality, then we have
obtained past due respect.

When the so-called government and political leaders
embrace civilized
brothers joined in arms, accept their differences,
and worked together for the
benefits of all the habitats and the entire country,
then we have overcome.

When the burning tires are place as a neckless
around a despised neighbor or a hate
political party opponent's neck be extinguishing,
then we have regained our humanity
and civility.

When the Gourde,
our national currency, no longer bedeviled, minimized,
shunned, and demonized by the United States central banks.
When the imbalance and disparity are no longer
five to one ratio to the US,
and the populous would accept their own currency
rather than carving and
confiscating and hoarding the US mighty dollar.
And our products and goods and exports are valuable,
sold, purchased, and on demand,
then we as a nation will be uplifted.

Tight Rope

Sneakers, black colored electrical lines,
sneakers hung high .

Hung them high,
hung them low.

Nikes, Pumas, my Adidas,
blow by blow.
Converse, Filas, and New Balance,
checked out from life too soon.
From rival gangs and illiteracy,
from the hypocrisy that densely justifies me.

Burden added, sorrow multiplied,
another project housing or ghetto negative statistic raises high.

Rising from the ashes of despair,
cruel, brutal, no respect or appreciation for life.

Not purchased by none, but claimed territory,
turf wars, homicides, and block parties are dumb.

Having respect in the hood,
reputation to uphold at all costs,
the supremacy of life.

Kamikazee pilots did not kill themselves,
but the enemy out there.

So, don't hang them high, don't hang them low.

Desperation of Despair

Our yellow butterflies are puny and fly lower
Not enough breeze or wind to make them fly high
like the mighty American eagle.
High above the clouds and mountains possibly
reaching their full potential.
Processes are given from above, that all butterflies are created
equal to be love and adore
Whiter green, blue, or monarch, noticeably seems by all.
Is it the unprepared Cocom, or perhaps the hasty caterpillar?
Or all lies, the lies and be trial that make them bitter.
Little mind. Little faith, little blossom bodies.

The Whaling Wall

What is that whaling so famous and admired by all?

Respected by many for its fulfillment of past prayed sentiments.

Niches carved in its Western façade hiding the faithful prayers
of all.

Many come from far away for a lifetime pilgrimage joyful journey.

Not hearing, learning,
and contemplating how to hate and kill the East and the West.

But for pure religious revenge, martyrdom,
and Jihad of what they stand for.

Standing strong of a mixture of mortar,
sweat, and blood; bounding all mankind to one
likely purposed.

Recognizing a higher power, request, petitions,
and fate and hope in the upcoming future.

Oasis of Love Too

Mountains of love,
breast peeking up like pyramids toward the sky.

Palm branches swinging on the wing, as her dark shiny hair
provides some shade.

Moist, juicy, and warmth,
is the feeling of the smooth but hard penetration?

She stands tall and firm as a palm Royal tree,
and like a palm tree in Lebanon.

Cry Little Boy Cry

Who will wipe away his desperate and sorrowful tears?
Cry little boy, cry
Who will take away his dark night fears?
Cry little boy, cry
Who will make things better?
Cry little booboo, cry
Who will stop the awful and bitter taste?
Cry little boy, cry
Who will say things will be better?
Cry little boy, cry
When the abuse continues at night,
Cry little boy, cry
When there is no way out, and he can't fight,
Cry little boy, cry
When he can't speak, and must keep it inside;
Cry little boy, cry
When no one will believe him or give him an ear,
Cry little boy, cry

Where can he go, for he is only five?
Cry little boy, cry
Where is the so call place, he can feel safe?
Cry little boy, cry
Where his embrace comes from, or complete solace,
Cry little boy, cry

What was is crime or infraction
Cry little boy, cry
What did he do to deserve this punishment?
Cry little boy, cry

Why did someone see it coming?
Cry little boy, cry
Why did someone quickly interfere?
Cry little boy, cry
Why did God just strike them dead?
So, he can have complete peace in his head.

Dr. Daniel Simon Pierre

False Identity

If I were God, I would not have created men,
For they are so foolish, so perverted, and so sinful.

If I were a bird, I would fly over people's heads,
And drop droplets of feces all over their cheep's hats,
old wigs, and faded toupees.

If I were a dog, I would go around and bite everyone
who did not give me a bone.

If I were a mosquito, I would only fly in the big cities
and bit only the wealthy people
and infect the affluent with Zika and the West Nile viruses.

If I were a woman, I would marry the richest man
in the world and divorce him for his money.

If I were gay, my lovers would only be pretty,
tall, and athletic-looking young man.

If I were a prostitute, I would infect
every unfaithful man with the HIV.

If I were a banker, I would not let poor folks
borrow money to buy weeds and cracks.

If I were white, I would live in the suburb,
attend private universities, and retire at forty.

If I were a judge, there would not be such thing

as death row; it will be a week row.

If I were the sun, I would burn all those
who do not use sunscreen or sunglasses.

If I were a baby, I would wet my diaper
50 times a day, would cry only at night,
and would drink five gallons of milk a day.

If I were a professional athlete,
I would be drug-free, stay out of trouble,
and don't forget where I came from.

If I were an ant, I would work destroying
people's manicured lawns and honeycake.

If I were a cow, I would urinate in the milk that I produce
so that children can get sick.

If I were a cop, I would shoot all the bad guys instantly,
and ascertain their innocence
after.

If I were poor, I would have eleven kids
and stay on welfare forever.

Self-Concept

When I look at myself,
I see someone good.
Not one without sin or blemish,
But one that can be understood

When I listen to myself,
I hear someone nice.
Not one with cold-blooded ice,
But one in which the feeling will last

When I smell myself,
I scent sweetness.
Not though the best,
But one which will not rest

When I taste myself,
I know I taste good.
Not a rotten yesterday's dish,
But some good fresh food

When I touch myself,
I feel warmth,
Not heat from a burning flame,
But overwhelming love from an overflowing heart

When I touch myself,
I feel the warmth coming from the earth's crust
Not negative or evil warmth,
But the real one straight from my heart.

In the Name of Nature

I am God who created you in my image
I am the sky who projects you from fallen aliens
I am the sun who warms the earth as it rotates on its axis
I am the clouds who give you a pillow as you fly over
I am the stars who lit your path shielding you from spiking rocks
I am the wind who brings you the pleasant fresh garden aroma
I am the trees who gives you a canopy for the midday sun
I am the dirt who grows your vegetation, dust to dust
I am the birds who start your day with an angelic melody
I am the rain who washes your sorrows and worries away
I am the sea who guides your large naval bodies
I am the water that you drink to say alive
I am the fish who you eat when you're tired of high-fat red meat
I am the cows who produce milk for your morning cereals
I am the spirit who keeps you going day after day
I am the fruits who smoothen you're going day after day
I am the earthquake, flood, and tornado who eliminates
corrupt men
I am the moon who lightens your way as you stroll to the park
I am the vegetable who provides fiber in your diet
I am the earth who provides you energy
I am who I am
In the name of nature
I am who I am
I am nature

Thanksgiving

Give thanks with a grateful heart
Give thanks to the Holy One
Give thanks because he has given, Jesus Christ his son
And now let the weak say I am strong
Let the poor say I'm rich
Because of what the Lord has done for us
And now let the sick say I'm whole, let the bound say I am free
Because of what the Lord has done for us
Give thanks to the Lord with praises and thanksgiving

Thank you, God, for creating me in your likeness
Thank you, God, for loving me despite my weakness
Thank you for giving me your only son to die for all my sins
Thank you for the Holy Spirit to guide me away from sins
Thank you for the gift of eternal life
Thank you for the precious breath of life
Thank you, God, for healing me and protecting me from diseases
Thank you, God, for my parents and my family too
Thank you, God, for everything that I have
Thank you, God, for all your blessing
Thank you, God, for all your miracles
Thank you, God, for peace of mind
Thank you, God, for your word of truth
Thank you, God, for my education
Thank you, God, for my salvation
Thank you, God, for saving my soul

On this day of Thanksgiving, turkey, stuffing, and trimming
I just want to thank you for the food on my table
Thank you for being there for me, and never forsaking me.

What Is Life

Is life just the big bang or the evolution theory?
Is life indeed creation made in the image of its creator?

Is life just s clump of cells, a mass of bacteria, or a spec of viruses?
Is it just ATP, mitochondria, DNA, RNA, and nuclei?

Is it just one day you are born, come to life, and die?
And the next you're old, frail, and can't even enjoy life

Is it just a passing fade, or is it to stay?
Is it just like the wind that we can feel and touch?

Is it purely materialistic processions, money, and wealth?
But when our eyes dim all things remain sadly behind

Life is fun, life is joy
Life is an underserving gift from the God-man above

Life is giving everything at any cost,
Yet, demanding nor expecting anything in return

Life is what you make out of it,
And not what you wish you had or could do with it

Life is short, changing, and unpredictable,
Life can also be fulfilling, stable, and pleasurable

Life is more than just work, bills, sadness, and sickness,
Life is friends, family, success, determination, and stamina
Life is a gift, life is love, and life is everlasting

Long Live Your Memory

Long live your memory
Forever I hope you live
I hardly knew you friend
I wanted to know you, cousin

You were full of life
You really loved life
Laughter erupted from your heart, and joy shined on your face
Sorrow and regret reflect on mine

You loved the beauty of all shapes and forms
You love beauty whichever way they come
Black, white Asians, you loved them all
I am proud to say that you were not a biggest

I know we don't always agree,
With a puppy in my bedroom, smoking, drinking, girls, and fun
But which didn't mean that I was better than you
Because you lived a happy life without reservation

Before it was your mother that I didn't know
Now it's you that I wish I knew
I hope you see her again someday
Somewhere nice, peaceful, and joyful

My mother is devasted
She remembered and was not close to her
She never goes one year without seeing you
She's your aunt, I guess she's always be

I hope you made peace with your maker
Long live your memory
Forever, I hope you live

White Waters

Yes, this is the White House;
White rivers, lakes, and ponds around it
Look I'm a Clintonite
Why should I care?
After all, I'm the president
And a very good swimmer
So, what if I cheated
No one got hurt

It was a long time ago
And I was a jerk
The governor, I was
Debate is my reply
I didn't know
I was going to make it to the top
Becoming a president right on the spot

Yes, I'm the smart-ass layer
Five feet tall, slim like a ruler
Blond I'm, my mother recalls
Shut up you too, before I drop the booms
So, what if the health plans do not work
The entire cabinet is full of jerks

Yes, I'm Chelsey "pretty girl" Clinton you can see
All the boys know me from my town
You know what I mean
Don't drop your tongue
Virgin you taught me I was

I'm a sorry big ass
I go to private school, but I 'm still a foul
Drugs and alcohol are all over the school

Afterword

Hello again, my dearest, faithful readers, and followers! Thanks to BooxAI and the great professional supporting collaborative team, I have other upcoming books and will continue to write and encourage the public until I run out of ideas.

After writing a series of poetry books (10 or 15) my goals, if the good Lord permits, are to write a cooking book (December), an exercise book (January), secular novels, and Christian motivation books in the near future, Sunday school books, sermons books, and a prayer book.

But in the meantime, please enjoy my first three submissions:

Book of Poetry (I Shall Rise)
Words from Above (Inspired)
Poetry of Love (I Love You)

Respectfully yours,

Dr. Daniel Simon Pierre
Writer / Poem
"The French Collection"